Alexa Märdian

Canadian or American. A small or an essential difference?

GRIN Publishing

Bibliographic information published by the German National Library:

The German National Library lists this publication in the National Bibliography; detailed bibliographic data are available on the Internet at http://dnb.dnb.de .

Imprint:

Print and binding: Books on Demand GmbH, Norderstedt Germany
ISBN: 978-3-656-91708-3

This book at GRIN:

http://www.grin.com/en/e-book/293935/canadian-or-american-a-small-or-an-essential-difference

Facharbeit

im Leistungskurs Englisch

Schuljahr 2013/14, 2.Halbjahr

Jahrgangsstufe Q1

Canadian or American - A small or an essential difference?

Alexa Maria Märdian

List of contents

1. Introduction

Canadian or American – A small or an essential difference? The question already implies that the subject of this thesis is focusing on culture and aspects of civil society rather than e.g. geographical differences.

Every country differs respectively its society from another but The United States and Canada are often assumed to be one of the most similar neighbours in the world. This is not surprising, due to the fact that 90 % of Canada's population lives within 120 kilometres of the US border.[1] So, is national identity really a matter of distance? As the years go by this lively-discussed issue has induced many sociologists and psychologists to research but a general consensus has never been found.

Canadians usually feel offended when they are named Americans and over the centuries Canada has tried to stress its unique identity and culture. Unfortunately, this phenomenon is often associated with the terms of "Canadian Nationalism" and "Anti-Americanism", or simply as Dr. Mark Snyder[2] defines it as *"identity by negation rather than affirmation"*[3].

But contrastingly and according to the "American Myths Survey", a co-operation between the Innovative Research Group and The Dominion Institute, de facto just 24% of the Canadians and 17% of the Americans feel that their values are becoming more similar. Moreover, 27% of the Canadians and 20% of the Americans actually feel that their particular values are becoming *"increasingly different"*.[4]

In order to analyze similarities and differences between the American and the Canadian civil society it is important to define culture at first. Culture, stated by Geert Hofstede[5], *"[...] is the collective programming of the mind distinguishing the members of one group from another."*[6]

This thesis is focusing on some main aspects influencing and coining society and culture, such as norms, values and history. Out of these aspects I selected categories which allow a basic functional differentiation of society.

---

[1] http://www.nationsencyclopedia.com/economies/Americas/Canada.html

[2] Head of the faculty of Psychology at the University of Minnesota (Canadian)

[3] Jonathan Wheelwright, "Nationalism", published August 8, 2005 http://www.unitednorthamerica.org/nationalism.htm

[4] Americ http://education.seattlepi.com/difference-between-canadian-american-university-degrees-3832.html an Myths Survey, publ. November 2005, p.7 https://www.historicacanada.ca/sites/default/files/PDF/polls/pollamericanmyths_en.pdf

[5] Dutch social psychologist and head of The Hofstede Centre, developed the "Dimensions of National Cultures"-Theory

[6] http://geert-hofstede.com/national-culture.html

2. Main part

2.1. Cultural diversity

The modern conception of "cultural diversity" generally describes differences among members and individuals of a common society based on their origin and ethnic background. A cultural diverse society contains a wide variety of races which usually includes different traditions among religions. Therefore, the term is often referred to as "multiculturalism" which is understood as an ideology of pluralism. However, broad differences exist in the way a country makes efforts to preserve and support its variety of cultures and reasons can be found in the particular history and experiences in former times.

Ethnic diversity makes up a substantial part of the Canadian as well as of the US-American society. Although, the population number is clearly different (317 million in the USA vs. 34.6 million in Canada), both communities contain a multitude of different cultures:

The largest proportion of Canada's citizen is white, 51% are descendants of the first settlers, so either of British Isles origin or French origin. About 6% are mostly Asian, African or Arab and 28% are from a mixed background. The inhabitants from the First Nations ancestry, called Aborigines, amount to about 2% of Canada´s total population. Though, it has to be noted, that they probably exceed this number because not all of them are officially registered.

Likewise in its bordering-country, most people are of white origin in the United States (79.96%).In addition, 12.85% of the U.S. population are dark-skinned, 4.43% are Asian, 0.18% are of Native Hawaiian origin or from other pacific islands. 1.61% are from a mixed background and Amerindians or Inuit (Alaska Natives) only make up 0.97%. The largest proportion of the U.S. citizens, which does not have native roots, is Hispanic and amounts to 15.1% of the total population. This percentage is included in the previous proportions because Hispanic inhabitants may be of any of these races.[1]

As already indicated, multiculturalism differs between the neighbouring-countries and the opposed situations are described by two famous metaphors.

---

[1] all figures are taken from: http://www.indexmundi.com/factbook/compare/united-states.canada

2.1.1. "Cultural mosaic" vs. "melting pot"

Canada is internationally recognized as one of the most welcoming and culturally diverse nations that lays emphasis on its concept of a "cultural mosaic". The metaphor describes a diversity of cultures which peacefully coexist in the same society and treat each other respectfully. Every culture can maintain its cultural heritage which carries along the individual language, belief and traditions, while shaping Canada's identity as a whole.

The issue of multiculturalism and a life in harmony began, when Canada became an official country in 1867 and people started to consider how to bring the founding-nations of the British Empire and France together[1]. From that time onwards the integration of different cultures, including the respective mother tongue as well as the traditions, was seen as duty. Today, it is referred to as the ideal of multiculturalism to respect Canadians of all backgrounds and ancestries.

This is contrasted to the US-American situation which is considered as a "melting pot". All immigrants are expected to give up their cultural identity and to adopt the American way of life in order to build a strong, homogenous and uniform democratic society.

This metaphor has also deep roots in the imagination of the American Dream. At the moment, when a person finally reached the boarder and arrived on Ellis Island to become a legal American citizen, he should throw away his sorrow and past to chase his own American Dream.

---

[1] Reva Joshee, Carla Peck, Laura Thompson, Ottilia Chareka, Alan Sears, "Multicultural education, diversity, and citizenship in Canada, published in February, 2012

http://www.intlalliance.org/fileadmin/user_upload/documents/Conference_2010/NP-CA.pdf

2.1.2. Multiculturalism policies

Although, the picture of the "melting pot" may be overage, it is still used when talking about US-American characteristics. Regarding the political area, it justifiably describes the situation of multiculturalism to some extent.

Both Canada and the United States make efforts to preserve their ethnocultural diversity but the reflection in the law differs.

During the premiership of Pierre Elliot Trudeau[1] from 1968-1979, multiculturalism became an official policy and in 1985 the "Canadian Multiculturalism Act" was passed, which defines *"[...] the diversity of Canadians [...] as a fundamental characteristic of Canadian society"*. Moreover, it *"recognized the importance of preserving and enhancing the multicultural heritage of Canadians"*, ensured the rights of Aboriginal people, provided English and French as the official languages and guaranteed equal rights regardless of the colour, religion and race.[2]

On the contrary, the United States does not make such constitutional affirmations. Even though there is the Department of Justice's Community Relations Service (CRS) to prevent racism, no official act for the preservation of the ethnic diversity has been enacted yet.[3]

Multiculturalism is adopted in the school education in both countries, but it varies in the U.S. because curriculums and requirements are regulated by each of the states. Therefore it is mostly just part of the education in areas which are close to borders and amount to large proportion of immigrants, for example Texas.[3]

In Canada all provincial or territorial ministries of education note ethnocultural diversity in the curriculums.

---

[1] 15th Prime Minister of Canada from Québec, * 1919-2000

[2] The Canadian Multiculturalism Act

http://laws-lois.justice.gc.ca/eng/acts/c-18.7/page-1.html

[3] Multiculturalism Policies in Contemporary Democracies

http://www.queensu.ca/mcp/immigrant/evidence/UnitedStates.html

On the federal level, the Council of Ministers of Education of Canada recognized it as being "[...] part of the daily classroom and school environment [...]"[1].From a very young age, Canadian school children are introduced to a broad variety of cultural traditions and customs which have become part of the Canadian identity and its mosaic. Both the government and society try to ensure that the traditions of all cultures are preserved and passed through from generation to generation.

---

[1]Multiculturalism Policies in Contemporary Democracies

http://www.queensu.ca/mcp/immigrant/evidence/Canada.html

2.2. Traditions and Customs

Canada and the United States are both very traditional nations which celebrate a broad range of holidays, for example memorial days or native festivities. The particular history of each country coined its heritage and gave rise to some distinctions.

Due to the fact that Canada's population is bilingual with a percentage of 74.5% English-speaking and 24.1% French-speaking citizens (mainly in Québec) [1], many Anglophone as well as Francophone traditions were preserved and carried on. Moreover, the Aboriginal culture still makes up a great part of the Canadian identity and the unique heritage of the First Nations, Inuit and Métis is celebrated on the National Aboriginal Day every year.

Just like Canada, the United States is very proud of its respective festivals. Compared to its neighbouring-country, the U.S. especially stresses its history and achievements of the past few centuries. In remembrance of Martin Luther King, leader of the African-American Civil Rights Movement, the third Monday in January was dedicated to him.[2] Furthermore, the U.S. places high value on the honour of military-service members by remembering those who died and celebrating all current military veterans. Memorial Day takes place on the last Monday in May and Veterans Day occurs on the 11th of November.[2]

Beside the individual holidays, the neighbouring-countries share a famous common festival which is also celebrated in some parts of Europe. On the surface, it seems to be similar but some differences developed bit by bit.

---

[1] figures of 2001, Office of the Commissioner of Official Languages, "Bilingualism in Canada", published in September 2005

http://www.ocol-clo.gc.ca/html/biling_e.php

[2] http://www.statesymbolsusa.org/National_Symbols/American_Hollidays.html

2.2.1. Thanksgiving

Thanksgiving is a traditionally day for family members and friends to come together and to review the past months while having a special meal. In Canada it occurs on the second Monday in October and lasts until the following Monday, whereas it is celebrated on the fourth Thursday in November until Sunday in the U.S.[1] This difference is a result of the particular origin of the festival.

Even before the first settlers arrived on Canada's coast, the Aboriginal people held various ceremonies "to celebrate the completion and bounty of the harvest"[2]. The early European tradition affected the festivity and people started "to thank for some special fortune"[2]. Later, when refugees of the U.S. Civil War escaped to the dominion, Thanksgiving took root and was celebrated annually. The British royal family also exerted a great influence and from then on the festival covered a specific royal topic. For many years, Thanksgiving fell on the same date as Remembrance Day until the Parliament declared in 1957: " A Day of General Thanksgiving to Almighty God for the bountiful harvest with which Canada has been blessed [...] to be observed on the second Monday in October."[3]

The origin of Thanksgiving in the United States is referred to the Pilgrims in Plymouth who are supposed to have celebrated it at first in the year 1621.[4] They thanked for the harvest and begged for rain to prevent droughts. Over the years, the religious significance increased and people started to go to church on every Thanksgiving.

The day differed from area to area but on the 26th of December in 1941 Franklin D. Roosevelt[5] signed a resolution which set Thanksgiving's current date.[6→]

---

[1] "Thanksgiving in America vs Thanksgiving in Canada"

http://www.diffen.com/difference/Thanksgiving_in_America_vs_Thanksgiving_in_Canada

[2] "Thanksgiving Day in Canada"

http://www.timeanddate.com/holidays/canada/thanksgiving-day

[3] "Thanksgiving"

http://www.craigmarlatt.com/canada/symbols_facts&lists/thanksgiving.html

[4] "Thanksgiving Day in the United States"

http://www.timeanddate.com/holidays/us/thanksgiving-day

[5] 32nd President of the United States (1933-1945), *1882-1945

2.3. Education

Beside its economic and political significance, education has a great impact on the country's particular society and culture. The more educated the individuals of a common society are, the more developed is their country. It is out of question that both Canada and the United States are highly-industrialized and most-developed nations but education also has the function of communicating respective values and transmitting the central heritage. Moreover, it informs about equal opportunities e.g. the access to universities in consideration of disparities in wealth and income.

Both countries are ranked among the best performing educational systems in several international surveys and their systems are quite similar; however, they differ in terms of funding, financing and teaching etc.

The Canadian schooling is tax-funded and the system is run by its ten provinces and three territories, whereas the U.S. Department of Education funds it south of the border. They both cover universal free elementary and secondary-schooling, which is compulsory for twelve years (expect in Québec for eleven years).Most Canadian universities are public institutions and the access is open to anyone, regardless of the income. And according to Ben Levin[1], Canada has a *"strong commitment [...] to equity for all population groups"*[2].

In contrast, the best universities in the U.S. are private and not affordable for those who do not have wealthy family backgrounds, fully-financed scholarships or certificates from private schools. In addition, the costs are generally much lower in Canada, with an average fee of about $5,000 per year, compared to the annual private-school tuition of estimated $32,100 in the U.S.[3]

[6←] Kimberly Ruble, "Thanksgiving: Why America celebrates this holiday", published November 28, 2013 http://guardianlv.com/2013/11/thanksgiving-why-america-celebrates-this-holiday/

[1] Canada Research Chair in Education Policy and Leadership at the Ontario Institute for Studies in Education

[2] "Comparing Canada and the U.S. on Education", published on April 4, 2011

http://blogs.edweek.org/edweek/futures_of_reform/2011/04/comparing_canada_and_the_us_on_education.html

[3] Kevin Wandrei, "Difference Between Canadian & American University Degrees", published in 2014

http://education.seattlepi.com/difference-between-canadian-american-university-degrees-3832.html

The gap between high and low performing Canadian students is smaller than average and according to the OECD PISA survey in 2012, the proportion of low performing 15-year-old students in mathematics amounted only to 11% versus 26% in the U.S.[1]With a proportion of 9%, compared to 15%[1] in the U.S., the socio-economic background also carries smaller weight in determining how Canadian students perform at school.

Teaching methods are generally the same in all parts of Canada, whereas the American curriculums and requirements are regulated by each of the fifty states. Furthermore, the content of teaching lays different focuses. The United States educates more towards national values and history, likewise in Germany. In the meantime, Canada's curriculum tends to be multi-ethnic oriented (see "cultural diversity").

---

[1]"Compare your country"

http://www.oecd.org/pisa/keyfindings/pisa-2012-results.htm

2.4. Health care

Healthcare is one significant aspect of the socioeconomic status of a country. Large differences in health care policy and its corresponding system are one indicator for the particular attitude of a society towards equal opportunities.

A collective health care system is typical for societies focussing on wealth distribution. The interdependence and well-being of the community are of paramount importance. One example is the equal access to medical treatment regardless of the income. In contrast, an individual health care system places high value on the freedom of choice, e.g. whether to be or not to be insured. It *"generally stresses the self-directed, self-contained, and comparatively unrestrained individual or ego"*[1].

Both Canada and the United States are closely involved in the delivery of healthcare but great differences exist between their funding mechanisms and health insurance:

The Canadian health care system is a universal single-payer system which means it is largely government-funded and mostly free. Most services are provided by private enterprises and it is usually referred to as "Medicare". It is based on the legal requirements constituted in the Canada Health Care Act of 1984, which assures that every legal citizen is covered through one of the 13 publicly-financed provincial or territorial plans. These plans all contain the same nationally defined basic standards for medical treatment as well as for coverage. Furthermore, the act regulates that all insured persons are completely insured, without any user fees or the necessity of making co-payments. In addition, Canada subsidizes medical service through global budgets for hospitals and according to the official definition *"[...] the principles governing our health care system are symbols of the underlying Canadian values of equity and solidarity"*.[2]

In contrast, the United States has a mixed public-private-system, colloquially called "Obamacare". Although, it is two-tiered likewise the Canadian, the access to each tier differs.

---

[1] Encyclopedia Britannica 6 (Holderness-Krasnoje), p.295

[2] Health Canada, http://www.hc-sc.gc.ca/hcs-sss/medi-assur/index-eng.php

The majority of the U.S. population does not have the possibility to access the public-provided tier, because it is mostly limited to specific groups of people, for example military-service members, disabled persons, children and some indigenous tribes. The secondary tier, including extra medical treatment among better quality as well as faster excess, is very expensive and just financeable for those who can afford high insurance contributions.

Therefore, 50 million people were not insured in 2009[1] and the per-capita spending on health care in 2007 was almost twice as high as in Canada (estimated US$7,250 vs. US$3850).[2] Published in 2010, the World Health Organization's rating of health care system performances ranked Canada 30th and the USA 37th, and the overall health of Canadians 35th compared to the health of US-Americans 72nd.[3]

Both systems are used as a model in the other country. The American system is used *"as a warning against increasing private sector involvement"*, meanwhile Canada's system is seen by the *"different sides of the ideological spectrum as either a model to be followed or avoided"*[4].

---

[1]Deborah White, "Pros & Cons of Government Healthcare

http://usliberals.about.com/od/healthcare/i/GovHealthCare.htm

[2]OECD Health Data 2010, see annex

[3]Rating of 191 nations in total

http://www.who.int/whr/2000/en/annex01_en.pdf

[4] "Health care in Canada vs. Health care in the United States

http://www.diffen.com/difference/Healthcare_In_Canada_vs_Healthcare_In_The_United_States

2.5. Gun Control

The view on federal gun control generally represents the particular attitude of a society in terms of tolerance and the need for security. Different levels of government responsibility usually imply either an advocating or antagonistic view on the government and its related institutions.

Exactly this difference in responsibility principally distinguishes the Canadian and American gun laws. Whereas gun control provisions are mainly set at the federal level in Canada, gun policies in the United States are primary set at the state level. Though, the federal government enacted a few laws, such as a requirement for firearm dealers to list the records of their sales, the US-American gun control still remains "a patchwork system of rules"[1]. Gun ownership is a privilege in Canada and many firearms are prohibited through the Firearms Act. Every gun owner needs a special licence to possess firearms and the transport is also restricted.

In contrast, gun ownership in the U.S. is seen as a basic right of all individuals *"[...] to keep and bear arms and should not be infringed."*[2] It is protected in the Second Amendment to the Constitution which was influenced by the English Bill of Rights of 1689. As a result of this law, the United States is being home of about 42.8% of all firearms, compared to 15.5% in Canada[3]. The English jurist Sir William Blackford[4] wrote in his "Commentaries on the Laws of England" that *"Self defense is justly called the primary law of nature, so it is not, neither can it be in fact, taken away by the laws of society."*[5]

---

[1] "An overview of Gun Control in US, Canada and Globally

http://guncontrol.ca/overview-gun-control-us-canada-global/

[2] an extract from the 2nd Amendment to the Constitution

http://www.law.cornell.edu/anncon/html/amdt2_user.html#amdt2_hd1

[3] http://guncontrol.ca/overview-gun-control-us-canada-global/

[4] English Tory politician of the eighteenth century

[5] "The Founders' Document on the Right to Keep and Bear Arms"

http://www.tysknews.com/Depts/2nd_Amend/rkba_docs_kw/political_philosophers.htm

This belief still coins a large part of the American society and moves gun lobbies like the NRA to fight against any restrictions of this right (*"The only thing that stops a bad guy with a gun is a good guy with a gun."*[1]).

The Canadian opinion about the loose gun control in its neighbouring country is fundamentally different. A writer of a famous Canadian magazine commented on this issue by asking, *"When are our American neighbors going to wake up and realize that gun production, gun rights and loose legislation are the real reason for these atrocities?"*[2]

According to David B. Kopel, one explanation for such a huge difference can be found in the history of the two neighbours. When the French pioneers explored Canada along the Atlantic coast they engaged in trade connections with the Paleo-Indians regarding the fur trade. The Hudson Bay Company's advertising slogan said *"never shoot your customers."* Due to this intercultural communication, the fear of the indigenous people was very small and the French had almost no reason for violence.

Opposed to the white inhabitants in the north, the English Pilgrims who began to settle on the eastern coast of North America wanted to stay and found colonies. They planned to farm and therefore, they had to fight against the Aboriginal tribes for the control of the land.[3]

---

[1] Wayne LaPierre, NRA Executive Vice President

Karen McVeigh, "NRA chief repeats call for 'good guys with guns' after navy yard shooting",

published September 22, 2013

http://www.theguardian.com/world/2013/sep/22/nra-wayne-lapierre-navy-yard-shooting

[2] Brian O'Neill, "Apples and oranges: The Canadian perspective on American gun control", published August 1, 2012

http://blog.thenewstribune.com/bluebyline/2012/08/01/apples-and-oranges-the-canadian-perspective-on-american-gun-control/

[3] "Canadian gun control: Should the United States look north for a solution to its firearm problems?", published in 1991

ttp://www.constitution.org/2ll/2ndschol/65kcgc.pdf

3. Conclusion

During my research on the Canadian and US-American civil society, I learned a lot about similarities and distinct aspects which differentiate both nations from each other. Although, some traditions and political opinions match superficially, differences arise on closer consideration.

In my opinion, the Canadian society tends to be collective and group-oriented. It places high value on the interdependence and well-being of the community, for example by creating equal opportunities. In contrast, individualism and the freedom of choice are of top priority in the United States. This American ideology is traceable to the three basic rights of "Life, liberty and the pursuit of happiness" which are enshrined in the Declaration of Independence. Moreover, Canadians are law-abiding and more supportive towards administrative institutions, while Americans advocate laissez-faire[1] and tend to be suspicious of federal control.

Another key difference is the European influence on Canada, especially from England and France. One half of Canada's government remained a constitutional monarchy and Queen Elizabeth is still the Head of State. Canada is not only member of the British Commonwealth of Nations but the British culture also influences the daily life, e.g. language. Furthermore, great parts are bilingual and French is provided as an official language of Canada by law.

To conclude, I can state that Americans and Canadians might share spare time activities, cuisine and the English language but core values differ essentially, coining two peerless identities and heritages.

---

[1] French term for "let it go" or "leave it"

4. List of references

American Holiday (Ed.): *American Holidays- United States National Holidays* [online] http://www.statesymbolsusa.org/National_Symbols/American_Hollidays.html 28.02.2014

Coalition for gun control (Ed.): *An Overview of Gun Control in Us, Canada and Globally* [online] http://guncontrol.ca/overview-gun-control-us-canada-global/ 26.02.2014

Cornell University Law School (Ed.): *CRS ANNOTATED CONSTITUTION Amend.2* [online] http://www.law.cornell.edu/anncon/html/amdt2_user.html#amdt2_hd126.02.2014

Diffen (Ed.): *Thanksgiving in America vs Thanksgiving in Canada* [online] http://www.diffen.com/difference/Thanksgiving_in_America_vs_Thanksgiving_in_Canada 28.02.2014

Diffen (Ed.): *Healthcare in Canada vs Healthcare in The United States* [online] http://www.diffen.com/difference/Healthcare_In_Canada_vs_Healthcare_In_The_United_States 15.02.2014

Ed. Encyclopedia of the Nations (Ed.): *Canada* [online] http://www.nationsencyclopedia.com/economies/Americas/Canada.html 17.02.2014

Government of Canada (Ed.): *Canadian Multiculturalism Act* [online] 1985 http://laws-lois.justice.gc.ca/eng/acts/c-18.7/page-1.html 19.02.2014

Griffiths, Rudyard and Greg Lyle: *Innovative Research Group/Dominion Institute Myth Survey* [online] November 2005 https://www.historicacanada.ca/sites/default/files/PDF/polls/pollamericanmyths_en.pdf 17.02.2014

Gwin, Robert P. (Ed.): *Britannica* Chicago 1990, volume 3, p.453, column 1, keyword "college"

Gwin, Robert P. (Ed.): *Britannica* Chicago 1990, volume 6, p.295, column 1, keyword "Indo-European languages"

Health Canada (Ed.): *Canada's Health Care System (Medicare)* [online] December 9, 2010 http://www.hc-sc.gc.ca/hcs-sss/medi-assur/index-eng.php 15.02.2013

Hofstede, Geert: *National cultural dimensions* [online] http://geert-hofstede.com/national-culture.html 17.02.2014

Indexmundi (Ed.): *United States vs. Canada- Country Comparison* [online] http://www.indexmundi.com/factbook/compare/united-states.canada 19.02.2014

Joshee, Reva and Carla Peck, Laura A. Thompson, Ottilia Chareka, Alan Sears: *Multicultural Education,Diversity, and Citizenship in Canada* [online] February 17-19, 2010 http://www.intlalliance.org/fileadmin/user_upload/documents/Conference_2010/NP-CA.pdf 19.02.2014

Kopel, David B.: *Canadian Gun Control: Should the United States look north for a solution to its firearms problem?* [online] 1991 ttp://www.constitution.org/2ll/2ndschol/65kcgc.pdf 26.02.2014

Levin, Ben: *Comparing Canada and the U.S. on Education* [online] April 4, 2011 http://blogs.edweek.org/edweek/futures_of_reform/2011/04/comparing_canada_and_the_us_on_education.html 30.03.2014

McVeigh, Karen: *NRA chief repeats call for 'good guys with guns' after navy yard shooting* September 22, 2013

http://www.theguardian.com/world/2013/sep/22/nra-wayne-lapierre-navy-yard-shooting 26.02.2014

OECD (Ed.): *PISA results 2012, Compare your country* 2012 http://www.oecd.org/pisa/keyfindings/pisa-2012-results.htm
(Please note that the "Compare your country"-table cannot be printed.)

Office of the Commissioner of Official Languages (Ed.): *Bilingualism in Canada* September 2005 http://www.ocol-clo.gc.ca/html/biling_e.php 19.02.2014

O'Neill, Brian: *Apples and oranges: The Canadian perspective on American gun control* August 1, 2012

http://blog.thenewstribune.com/bluebyline/2012/08/01/apples-and-oranges-the-canadian-perspective-on-american-gun-control/ 18.02.2014

Ruble, Kimberly: *Thanksgiving: Why America celebrates this holiday* November 28, 2013 http://guardianlv.com/2013/11/thanksgiving-why-america-celebrates-this-holiday/ 28.02.2014

Queen's University (Ed.): *Multiculturalism Policies in Contemporary Democracies* http://www.queensu.ca/mcp/immigrant/evidence/UnitedStates.html 19.02.2014 http://www.queensu.ca/mcp/immigrant/evidence/Canada.html 19.02.2014

Time and Date (Ed.): *Thanksgiving in Canada* www.timeanddate.com/holidays/canada/thanksgiving-day 28.02.2014

Time and Date (Ed.): *Thanksgiving in the United States*

www.timeanddate.com/holidays/us /thanksgiving-day 28.02.2014

Tysknews (Ed.): *The Founders' Document on the Right to Keep and Bear Arms* http://www.tysknews.com/Depts/2nd_Amend/rkba_docs_kw/political_philosophers.htm 26.02.2014

Wandrei, Kevin: *Differences between Canadian & American University Degrees* 2014 http://education.seattlepi.com/difference-between-canadian-american-university-degrees-3832.html 30.02.2014

Wheelwright, Jonathan: *Nationalism* August 8, 2005 http://www.unitednorthamerica.org/nationalism.htm 15.02.2014

White, Deborah: *Pros & Cons of Government Healthcare* http://usliberals.about.com/od/healthcare/i/GovHealthCare.htm 14.02.2014

World Health Organization: *The World Health Report 2000* http://www.who.int/whr/2000/en/annex01_en.pdf 14.02.2014

5. Annex*

In reference to “Health Care”, p.13

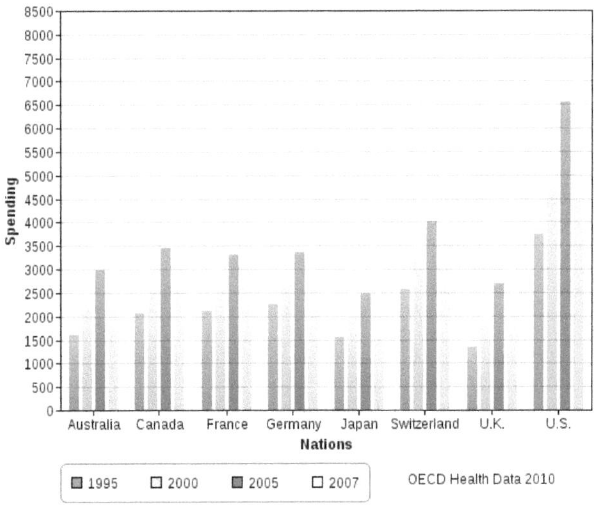

Source: http://en.wikipedia.org/wiki/Health_care_system_in_Japan

* All documents are alphabetically sorted by the surname of the author/editor.